Gold Coast

a panoramic gift book

Steve Parish

Contents

Gold Coast

from the heart

The Gold Coast is one of the world's most popular holiday destinations. Its beaches and resort towns stretch from Sanctuary Cove in the north to Coolangatta in the south and it enjoys sunshine almost all year round, luring holidaymakers from across the globe. A swag of popular theme parks, superb shopping and world-class restaurants and accommodation only add to the Gold Coast's allure.

However, glorious beaches and glamorous resorts aside, it is also blessed with wondrous natural habitats and richly productive farming land in the hinterland. The World-Heritage-listed Central Eastern Rainforest Reserves and the cascading waterfalls in numerous national parks are natural highlights. I hope this book gives you a sense of the magic of the Gold Coast.

Steve Parish

City for Surfers

a modern metropolis on the beach

In the 1950s, the Gold Coast was little more than a few sleepy collections of fibro beach houses gathered around local pubs and grocery stores. Visitors camped or stayed in old-style boarding houses, and many avid anglers and Brisbane families built "beach shacks".

In the 1960s, Australia's surf culture really took off, and so began the Gold Coast's astronomical growth – first at Surfers Paradise, and then right along the beaches to the Queensland–New South Wales border. Ever higher and more elaborate buildings rose on the skyline; the meandering channels of the Nerang River were turned into canals; and a shoppers' and surfers' paradise was built. Today, this modern, vibrant conglomeration of seaside suburbs attracts more than 10 million visitors a year to its sunny beaches, theme park attractions and luxurious hotels and apartments. Its growth and popularity goes ever onward.

Looking south along The Spit, over the Sea World theme park and the Broadwater, to the skyscrapers that line Main Beach and Surfers Paradise.

The impressively tall Q1 building towers over Surfers Paradise.

Both backpackers and billionaires are lured to the seaside alfresco venues and the popular strip of beach along The Esplanade at Surfers Paradise.

Looking across the Nerang River and the canal suburbs to Surfers Paradise and Southport.

Waves lap at endless stretches of golden beach — just one of the many enticements to holiday on the Gold Coast.

Pleasure craft, from luxury yachts to deep-sea fishing boats, jostle for mooring space in one of Australia's premier boating playgrounds.

Days on the beaches begin with a beautiful sunrise.

Shadows lengthen as bathers squeeze the last rays of heat from the day.

Beach Bliss

on the sands and in the waves

The Gold Coast's beaches are world famous. Swathes of golden sand invite walkers, joggers, sunbathers and beach cricketers to enjoy the endless summer sun. Families frolic in the shallows and swimmers throng between the flags while surf lifesavers keep guard. Out beyond the breakers, surfers bob, waiting for the perfect tube, and along the beach anglers cast their lines, hoping for a good catch.

A sandcastle architect works in the midday sun.

Strolling along the tideline, feeling the sand underfoot, is a daily pleasure for many residents and holidaymakers.

The surf culture draws many board-riders to the Gold Coast.

Surf lifesavers freely give their time to protect swimmers.

Windsurfers strain against a sharp breeze.

A power boat cruises on the Broadwater in front of Marina Mirage.

Triathlons and surf lifesaving competitions are common on the Gold Coast.

Some of the best surf breaks in the world are found on the Gold Coast.

Twilight paints the beaches fronting the Pacific Ocean.

The peaceful, well-protected Broadwater is always popular with windsurfers.

Houseboats, monohulls and catamarans make their way along the Broadwater.

The Broadwater

a water sports playground

Protected to the south by The Spit, and to the north by the offshore bulk of South Stradbroke Island, the calm expanse of the Broadwater provides a pleasant harbour for boaters and a safe enclave for water sports enthusiasts, including windsurfers, parasailers, jet-ski riders and kite surfers.

The Broadwater stretches north from Southport past the suburbs of Labrador, Biggera Waters, Anglers Paradise, Runaway Bay, Hollywell and Paradise Point and provides access to the Gold Coast Seaway, where charter boats and game fishing vessels plough their way through the chop to fish the Pacific Ocean reefs and depths beyond.

Cartoon characters greet visitors to Warner Bros. Movie World.

Kids enjoy the Speedcoaster ride and the safe waters of Buccaneer Bay at Wet 'n' Wild.

Year-round Fun

from theme parks to super cars

The Gold Coast boasts almost every form of fun, from Jupiters Casino to Ripley's Believe It or Not Museum. Every month has its highlights, with the Magic Millions horse races in January and the Indy car races in October both being extremely popular. Theme-park fun is non-stop, whether at the Australian Outback Spectacular, Wet 'n' Wild, Warner Bros. Movie World, or at the ever-popular Sea World and Dreamworld.

Australian Outback Spectacular — a dinner show with outback music drama and action.

Gold Coast streets roar with excitement at Indy 300 in October.

Dreamworld

Billed as "So many worlds in one", Dreamworld offers activities for even the most unshockable thrill-seeker. Jaw-dopping rides, such as the Tower of Terror, the Giant Drop and The Claw, excite adrenalin junkies, while exotic animal shows, featuring the graceful and powerful Bengal Tiger, entertain nature lovers. For a more relaxed time, vistors can cruise along the "Murrissippi" River on a paddlewheeler or enjoy one of many live shows.

Take a relaxing cruise on Dreamworld's *Captain Sturt* Paddlewheeler.

A regal Bengal Tiger, one of the residents of Dreamworld's Tiger Island.

Sea World

Sea World, on The Spit at Main Beach, is one of the Gold Coast's most popular theme parks. The fun-filled mix of attractions includes close encounters with sea creatures, thrilling roller-coasters and wildlife shows, including the Dolphin Cove Show and Waterski Wipeout. Popular residents are the Bottlenose Dolphins, the Polar Bears, which frolic in their specially built Arctic summer playground of Polar Bear Shores, and the fearsome underwater predators of Shark Bay.

Bottlenose Dolphins at Dolphin Cove delight visitors by happily performing various stunts.

Polar Bear Shores, one of the many attractions at Sea World.

Shopping

something for everyone

Everyone shops on the Gold Coast! Such is the laid-back pace of life that it is a delight to wander through Cavill Mall and the various boutiques and arcades, spoilt for choice for things to buy, rather than having to hurry from place to place in the midst of the frenzied day-to-day life of Australia's capital cities. Shopping centres on the Coast cater to every possible whim and are equal to any in the world for range and price.

Marina Mirage on The Spit.

Pacific Fair, on the highway at Broadbeach.

Australia Fair at Southport.

The Chevron Renaissance centre at Surfers Paradise.

Hope Island resort, at the northern end of the Gold Coast, is an affluent enclave.

Canals along the Nerang River allow for the private mooring of luxury vessels.

Lavish Lifestyles

on canals and in skyscrapers

The Gold Coast is one of the most affluent cities in Australia, which is reflected by the glitz and glamour of its major town centres, with their sky-scraping structures of gleaming glass and steel rising above boutique fashion stores and world-class restaurants. Many of these five-star highrises overlook the water, and catch the sea breeze which sets lavish yachts at private moorings bobbing on the gentle waters.

However, the Gold Coast is more than just a lifestyle choice for the rich and famous; hundreds of thousands of people live and work in and around this sunny city, contributing to the arts, manufacturing, primary production, business and communications sectors.

Leisure boats also harbour in waterways that surround identikit resort-style apartments.

The Gold Coast's famous skyline is punctuated with skyscrapers overlooking the Pacific Ocean.

Towering above the sands and shining against the eternal blue sky are highrise buildings in a multitude of styles and textures.

Architectural artworks on the Gold Coast come in an assortment of pastel colours and supply spectacular ocean views.

Views over North Burleigh and Burleigh Beach to Burleigh Head National Park.

Burleigh Heads

where beach meets national park

South from the glamour of Surfers and Broadbeach, life takes on a slightly more relaxed pace at Burleigh Heads. This is the territory of committed surfers and beach lovers, but the area around the green bulk of Burleigh Head offers more natural habitat than can be found further north. The national park and Tallebudgera Creek provide a refuge for many birds and animals.

Sun-worshippers relax on Burleigh Beach.

Burleigh Head National Park, on the north bank of Tallebudgera Creek, provides sanctuary for coastal wildlife.

Wildlife Parks

Currumbin Sanctuary & Fleay's Wildlife

Currumbin Wildlife Sanctuary and the David Fleay Wildlife Park both provide visitors with the chance to see, hear and, in some cases, touch native Australian animals and birds. Both are important wildlife research and rehabilitation centres. Currumbin Sanctuary has been run by the National Trust since Alex Griffiths deeded it to the Queensland branch. David Fleay's Wildlife Park was the first to breed Platypuses successfully in captivity.

Boardwalks throughout the park allow visitors to view the animals.

Koalas are among the most popular residents.

Clockwise from top: Scenes from Currumbin Wildlife Sanctuary – the train takes a 2-kilometre tour of the park; feeding the Rainbow Lorikeets; an encounter with a young Eastern Grey Kangaroo.

Currumbin

beach breaks

Any day that the surf is up, the waters of the southern Gold Coast will be filled with riders paddling beyond the break, floating and chatting while they wait for a wave, or surging beachward once their exhilarating ride has arrived. The names of these beaches are fixed in Australian surfing legend: Burleigh, Currumbin, Greenmount, Snapper Rocks, Kirra, Duranbah.

Elephant Rock buffers the Currumbin Surf Lifesaving Club.

Surfers paddle at The Alley, just off Currumbin Rock, awaiting the next big wave.

The view northward from Elephant Rock in the early light of dawn.

Currumbin morning

Early morning touches the shores of Currumbin with romance and mystery. The dawn light, with its misty pinks and mauves, softens the outlines of apartment buildings, office towers and hotels on the horizon beyond Elephant Rock.

Later, the clear light brings forth the full, sparkling colours of water and sand: azure, green, turquoise, aquamarine and gold surround Currumbin Rock as it juts out into the Pacific Ocean.

Currumbin Rock at the mouth of Currumbin Creek.

Coolangatta

the State's most southerly seaside town

Coolangatta just north of the Tweed River has a nearby twin city, Tweed Heads, nestled on the river just south of the Queensland State border. Coolangatta's quiet, north-facing beaches, which are protected from southerly winds, are now frequented by families, but in the 1950s Greenmount Beach in Coolangatta was the most popular spot for young adults, thanks to its famed beach parties.

Captain Cook Memorial Lighthouse, Point Danger.

A sculpture of an eagle gazes out to sea on the foreshore.

Point Danger, named by Captain James Cook in 1770, juts out to sea north of the Tweed River mouth. Rainbow Bay and Greenmount Beach lie on the north of the point.

Coolangatta and Greenmount Beaches.

Tranquil Greenmount Beach.

Tweed Heads, NSW, with Point Danger on the right and Jack Evans Boat Harbour on the left.

The Hinterland

the green behind the gold

Just behind the Gold Coast are the wilderness wonders of the Gold Coast Hinterland, including the Darlington and McPherson Ranges and the Lamington Plateau. Within these rugged mountains lie the Lamington, Springbrook and Border Ranges National Parks, all part of the Central Eastern Rainforest Reserves of Australia, a listed site on the World Heritage Register. These parks are refuges for a wealth of rare plant and animal species.

Scattered through the mountains are historic townships such as Tamborine and Beechmont, cool, idyllic destinations in the depth of summer's heat.

The Coomera and Nerang Rivers have their headwaters in the ranges, where waterfalls plunge down rainforest-clad cliffs. Many of the wider valleys, like Numinbah, are richly productive farming areas.

The Gold Coast skyline seen over the greenery of the Lamington Plateau.

Mt Tamborine

Tamborine Mountain, 30 kilometres inland from the Gold Coast, is a plateau that formed from an outpouring of lava from Mt Warning. Several small villages combine to make up the town of Tamborine, and they are interspersed within twelve separate reserves that together make up Tamborine National Park. The area was first settled by timber-getters and a sawmill was built at Cedar Creek in the 1860s. Tamborine village itself was established around 1878. Among the many points of interest are an increasing number of boutique wineries, galleries and Bed & Breakfast romantic hideaways.

Above, left and right: Two examples of Tamborine's quaint architecture.

Clockwise from top: Tamborine Mountain Heritage Centre; more than a dozen galleries, antique stores and nurseries make Tamborine village worth a visit.

National Parks

misty, mossy retreats in the mountains

In the forests of Lamington and Springbrook National Parks, the chuckle of running water is an ever-present background to a chorus of bird song.

Labyrinthine fungi grow on fallen logs and tree bases, gradually breaking down the wood and turning it back into food for newly shooting trees and ferns. Mosses and lichens spread across the moist surfaces of rocks and tree trunks, and epiphytic ferns hang from branches, shivering with the air's movement. In Lamington National Park, Antarctic Beech forests include trees that were young two thousand years ago.

In the forested national parks, male bowerbirds entice females to their bower with elaborate courtship displays and those who are lucky enough may catch a glimpse of the rare Albert's Lyrebird or hear its mimicking calls.

Chalahn Falls, Lamington National Park, tumble onto moss-covered rocks.

Antarctic Beech forest has grown here for thousands of years.

Clear mountain water plunges into a forest-fringed pool in Tamborine National Park.

Buttress roots spread over a track in the Palm Grove section of Tamborine National Park.

Red-necked Pademelons graze outside the forest, but usually hide in dense undergrowth during daylight hours.

An Agile Wallaby with a large joey in the pouch.

Bird's Nest Ferns catch falling leaves in their outspread "nests".

Light shines through the delicate gills of a fungus.

Boardwalks through the rainforest on O'Reilly's Tree Top Walk bring visitors closer to nature.

Elabana Falls cascade over rocks in Lamington National Park.

bright birds of the forest

Some of the small, shy birds of the forest have muted plumage of grey, brown and cream and are hard to spot, despite their loud, clear songs. But many others, especially the vividly apparelled parrots, are decked in bright colours that seem like the rashest advertisement of their presence. Oddly, however, the vibrant colours can be difficult to spot amongst the deep green of the forest, and the bird's movement is often the only thing that makes its location obvious. In some areas, parrots have learned to value being offered seeds by humans and have become quite tame.

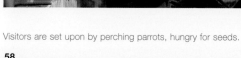

Visitors are set upon by perching parrots, hungry for seeds.

A Crimson Rosella stretches on its perch.

The brightly plumed, scarlet and emerald, male Australian King-Parrot.

Male Regent Bowerbirds inhabit the forest.

Morans Falls, one of the most impressive waterfalls in full flood, seen from Morans Falls Lookout.

Within the forest every surface is covered by plants, each with something to offer other life forms.

Natural Bridge, where a waterfall tumbles through rock into a spacious cave, the roof of which glimmers with glow worms at night.

Springbrook National Park

Springbrook National Park is almost 3000 hectares of rainforest, open forest and montane heath clothing spectacular cliffs and gorges carved by flowing water and volcanic activity over the aeons.

Rare birds and butterflies inhabit the forest, while glittering dragonflies dance on the water of forest streams where long-legged, goggle-eyed frogs live and breed.

Springbrook is part of the mountainous Scenic Rim, perched high above the coastal plain near the Queensland–New South Wales border. The park has plenty of graded walking tracks and picnic areas, a few of which are suitable for wheelchairs and strollers.

Purlingbrook Falls plunge into Springbrook National Park.

From an early age, Steve Parish has been driven by his undying passion for Australia to photograph every aspect of it, from its wild animals and plants to its many wild places. Then he began to turn his camera on Australians and their ways of life. This body of work forms one of Australia's most diverse photographic libraries. Over the years, these images of Australia have been used in thousands of publications, from cards, calendars and stationery to books – pictorial, reference, guide and children's. Steve has combined his considerable talents as a photographer, writer, poet and public speaker with his acute sense of needs in the marketplace to create a publishing company that today is recognised worldwide.

Steve's primary goal is to turn the world on to nature, and, in pursuit of this lifelong objective, he has published a world-class range of children's books and learning aids. He sees our children as the decision makers of tomorrow and the guardians of our heritage.

Published by Steve Parish Publishing Pty Ltd
PO Box 1058, Archerfield, Queensland 4108 Australia
© copyright Steve Parish Publishing Pty Ltd
ISBN 174021917 1
10 9 8 7 6 5 4 3 2 1
Photography: Steve Parish
Additional photography: p. 24 (left) Movie World; p. 24 (right) Wet 'n' Wild; p. 25 (left) Outback Spectacular; p. 25 (right) Dale Blackmore, Australian Picture Library; p. 27 Sea World.
Text: Wynne Webber & Karin Cox, SPP
Design: Leanne Nobilio, SPP & Gill Stack SPP
Editing: Ted Lewis, SPP & Michele Perry, SPP
Production: Tiffany Johnson, SPP
Front cover: The Gold Coast, seen across The Spit and the Broadwater.
Title page: Surfers off Currumbin Beach.
Printed by South China Printing
Prepress by Colour Chiefs Digital Imaging, Brisbane, Australia
Produced in Australia at the Steve Parish Publishing Studios

Steve Parish™
PUBLISHING

FOR PRODUCTS
www.steveparish.com.au
FOR LIMITED EDITION PRINTS
www.steveparishexhibits.com.au
FOR PHOTOGRAPHY EZINE
www.photographaustralia.com.au

online